Above, top to bottom: Red Kangaroo, Laughing Kookaburras and Koala – symbols for Australia's wildlife.

THE EXCEPTIONAL AUSTRALIANS

Australia does not have vast herds of wild, cloven-hoofed animals roaming its plains, nor does it have large roving carnivores like big cats, however it does have its own collection of extraordinary wild creatures.

Let's face it, wildlife with names like – Potoroo, Bettong, Echidna, Platypus, Bilby, Bandicoot, Numbat, Planigale, Possum, Phascogale, Quoll, Koala, Galah, Wallaby, Dingo, Kangaroo, Kookaburra and Wombat must have something going for them!

There are many native Australian animals that we usually only see in picture books, rarely in the wild. The reason is simple. Most are active only at night and even under the cloak of darkness, very secretive and timid.

You will see them though, if you spend time in the bush, in the right places, at the right time of day and you are prepared to be very quiet.

Particularly good places to observe many of Australia's more unique and generally unapproachable wildlife is in and around National Parks, particularly camping areas. In such places they have usually become tolerant of people and will often allow you to approach – particularly possums, wallabies, kangaroos, and some parrot species. I have even had rarely seen Quolls dance between my legs while I was sitting beside a camp fire – one even had the hide to dive headlong into my freshly brewed hot chocolate!

Above, top left and clockwise: Laughing Kookaburra; Quoll; Emu; Koala; Brush-tailed Phascogale; Tasmanian Devil; Ghost Bat; Frill-necked Lizard. Centre: Bilby.

Common Wombat.

THE KOALA – AN INTERNATIONAL HERO!

I will be the first to admit that until I had come into personal physical contact with a Koala I had considered them as rather boring animals. After all, all they do is sleep and eat! Of course what many of us do not realise is that the Koala, like many other marsupials, is only active at night. My first physical contact was with a young Koala that had just left its mother's pouch and I was hooked in about two seconds flat. I found its endearing stare impossible to resist.

Of course the effect that the Koala has had on people all over the world is quite stunning. In Japan people flock to a special Koala Zoo in millions every year. Visiting Koalas in Zoos and fauna parks is almost like some sort of religious experience for most people; maybe the Koala carries some sort of genetic memory jog that invokes in us the desire to reach out and hold or cuddle what symbolises a defenceless baby?

Having become something of an international hero, the Koala has also evolved as a symbol for the protection of its habitat and that of course is what conservation is about. Maybe now we can link King Parrots to rainforests, Red Kangaroos to arid lands, Australian Pelicans to wetlands and so on.

Above: The International Hero.

Stand up the hero!

BIRDS – SYMBOLS OF FREEDOM

There are kinds that swim underwater, others that can't fly but they can run at 50 kmph! Still others spend their day riding columns of air, some live on remote wind-swept offshore islands, in dark mosquito-filled mangrove swamps, in bushlands, rainforests... in fact every Australian habitat has its own bird communities. Some habitats even go so far as having birds that are specific to them; the Chestnut Quilled Rock Pigeon of the Kakadu National Park escarpment country occurs nowhere else in the world!

There are about 750 different kinds of birds known to inhabit Australia and out of that number about 350 are unique to Australia.

Perhaps the most dramatic of all Australian bird species are the parrots; there are around 50 different kinds. What sets the parrots apart from most other groups of birds are their vivid colours, the fact that many species form huge flocks, and most certainly the noise they make, and that humans enjoy their "comical behaviour".

The most awe-inspiring thing about birds is that most can fly and for that reason they have always symbolised freedom of the spirit to man. For me, it is always an immense privilege to share a fleeting, sometimes seemingly confidential, moment with such an intensely living fellow being.

Above, top to bottom: Brolga; Pelicans and Honeyeater.

BIRD DREAMING

Flying
deep inside a forest,
along a wave tossed shore,
a plain that's endless or a tiny island way offshore,
anywhere you seem to look there's
secrets in those flying feathers,
spirits filling air.

Flaming
red and crimson-blue,
yellow eye-to-eye with curious knowing stare,
seems to want to tell me something
'bout some mystery lost in air.

Floating
'round fleeting confidential moments,
keeping secrets as they ruffle feathers,
give a nervous flutter, preen, poke, pry,
then suddenly they're gone
a mystery where!

Black Swan and cygnets – elegant Australians.

OF ELEGANCE AND ENTERTAINMENT

Estuaries, reed-fringed and placid, can present wonderfully tranquil experiences. Generally protected by dunes or high banks, estuarine waters are usually still, and they are also rich with food for dozens of water and sea bird species which may come in thousands depending on the season and locality.

Two of the most endearing birds to be found along temperate estuaries are the Australian Pelican and the Black Swan; birds totally different in both character and appearance.

Pelicans are particularly interesting characters to watch. They form flocks and it is the interactions between birds that provide the entertainment. For example they clamp their giant bills over each others' necks; yawn in a most amusing manner; clap their membranes as though approving another bird's performance; preen in a multitude of ungainly postures and they seem to love holding conferences of seemingly great importance.

The Black Swan embodies grace and great dignity. Little rivals the poetic form and motion of Black Swans swimming on tranquil water, their elegant shape mirrored on the blue-green surface. Accompanied by a string of cygnets a parent bird puffs with seeming pride as it paddles back and forth with little apparent effort.

Above: Australian Pelicans.

THE BLACK-AND-WHITE BRIGADE

When I look up the word courage in my Thesaurus I find such words as dauntlessness, guts, heart, mettle, pluck, resolution, spirit and spunk – it should also include "Willie Wagtail"!

The metallic, two-syllable rattling cry of the Willie Wagtail when distressed is familiar to anyone who has spent time listening to the sounds of the Australian bush. When you hear this cry it is fairly certain that this little bundle of feathered courage is trying desperately to challenge a territorial intruder of one sort or another whether it be wild cattle, buffalo, Wedge-tailed Eagles, Kookaburras, Kangaroos, or even people if they happen to get in the Wagtails' way!

Apart from the Willie Wagtail the black-and-white brigade has many members – there's the sweet singing Butcherbird, the ever-staring Pee-wee, the urban invading Magpie and that marauding bush larrikin the Currawong.

What the black-and-white brigade may lack when compared with more colourful groups of birds, they certainly make up for in character. As a group they are as Australian as the Koala and the Red Kangaroo.

Top row: Willie Wagtail attacking a Black-shouldered Kite. Second row: Willie Wagtail, Currawong and Magpie. Bottom row: Crow, Pee-wee and Crow.

Pied Butcherbird.

Sulphur-crested Cockatoo.

Australian Emu.

Jacky Winter.

Grey Kangaroo.

Northern Hairy-nosed Wombat.

DISCOVERING AUS

PARROTS – THOSE CIRCUS ACROBATS

Possibly the best known of all parrots is the Sulphur-crested Cockatoo. For me one of the most delightful things about this particular bird is the sounds it makes, which vary from raucous cries to gentle murmurs. On one occasion I camped under tall gum trees and was lulled to sleep by the collective murmurings of Cockatoos. At dawn I awoke to hear rain gently falling on the tent. When I got up I discovered that the rain was in fact gum leaves, each neatly stripped off by the 100 or so Cockatoos camped above me.

The Sulphur-crested Cockatoo and other related parrots are without doubt Australia's most popular birds. There are more than 50 different kinds, 48 of which are found nowhere else in the world, and what really sets them apart from other families of birds is their flashy plumage and the fact that many species form large and often very noisy flocks. Some, like the King Parrot, Crimson Rosella, Scaly-breasted and Rainbow Lorikeets have been semi-domesticated around suburban gardens and in popular nature parks, thus enabling close contact which, in turn, has further promoted their popularity worldwide.

Above, top left and clockwise: Rainbow Lorikeet; Galahs; King Parrot; Scaly-breasted Lorikeet; Crimson Rosellas bathing; Musk Lorikeet.

Crimson Rosella.

a.

Red-necked Wallaby.

Laughing Kookaburra.

Frill-necked Lizard.

TRALIA'S WILDLIFE

Steve Parish

King Parrot.

KANGAROO CAPERS

Having very acute hearing, sight and smell, kangaroos and wallabies are past masters at their own survival, so hunting them with a camera is a stimulating and challenging pastime.

Stalking is particularly exciting if there is good cover to play your hide-and-seek game. If the 'roo looks up at you while you are stalking don't give up, you may still bluff the animal into going back to its feeding or grooming by remaining absolutely still.

I am always fascinated by the manner in which the kangaroo uses its ears, like a pair of independently operating radar sensors. Even when the animal appears relaxed, the ears are scanning for even the slightest sound.

There are lots of other fascinating things to observe about kangaroo behaviour: there's boxing, grooming, sunbaking, caring for their pouched young and probably the most fascinating of all, their ability to "fly" with the wind!

Above, top left and clockwise: Red Kangaroo; Pretty-face Wallaby; Wallaroo; Boxing Grey Kangaroos and Red Kangaroo with joey.

Agile Wallaby – in search of an itch.

THE ELEGANT DINGO

It was around midnight. The air was warm, the moon full. We had had a very late meal and I had taken my cup of coffee for a walk into the sand dunes for a little quiet relaxed contemplation about what had been an eventful day.

I was sitting staring at the moon when I heard a very gentle whimper behind me. When I turned I got the shock of my life. There, standing no more than three metres away, was the most beautiful, proud-looking Dingo bitch I had ever seen. We stared at each other. Then, suddenly, she had company; two tiny golden Dingo pups, standing very close by her side. All three stared at me. I froze, hoping the moment would last and, like any photographer, cursing that one moment in the day when I did not have a camera!

Scientists believe that the Dingo was introduced to Australia by Aborigines around 3,000 years ago and for that reason there are some who would argue that the Dingo is not a true native animal. However, today the Dingo is a highly successful animal and it may be found in any habitat right across the length and breadth of Australia.

Above: An elegant Dingo.

Chasing Silver Gulls.

TUNING IN TO REPTILES

We had launched our small boat off the banks of a wide tropical river and within moments my old aboriginal friend whispered, "dem one over dere" and, looking along his finger, I stared into the gnarled and twisted branches of the verging swamp. Nothing! I was too embarrassed to show my inability to see so I gave the customary mumble of seeming appreciation. We pushed on, seconds later, "nother one over dere". This time I could just see the eyes of a very large Saltwater Crocodile protruding from among the broken drifting branches.

I was learning, first hand, that to find these reptiles, in fact any reptiles, I needed to tune in my eyes, my body and my spirit to the landscape.

For most people, reptiles are a group of animals to fear, to draw away from in disgust. While I certainly do not expect you to go and throw your arms around a crocodile or, for that matter, walk bare footed where Death Adders abound, I would point out that very, very few reptiles are in fact dangerous to man. For example, out of 130 or so known snakes, all of which are poisonous, only 20 are dangerous to humans. The old adage applies – "if crocodiles had evolved to eat people, then they would have been extinct thousands of years ago". However, if you go swimming with them be prepared to be mistaken for a hearty meal!

Above, top to bottom: Freshwater Crocodile; Saltwater Crocodile and Freshwater Crocodile.

Green Python – harmless to man.

THE POSSUM PUZZLE

Some years ago I was given the challenging assignment of photographing possums among the beautiful tropical rainforests of northern Queensland, an area rich in possum numbers and species. My host was a man who had spent most of his life unravelling the puzzles that surround possums, an enduring task as all possums are active by night, which meant that while everyone was going to bed John Winter was going to work.

Night-active possums have particularly large reflective retinas in their eyes, which gather what light is available. By using powerful spotlights and by holding the light-source level with the human eye, it is possible to detect the reflective eye-shine of a possum from over 100 metres away.

On the very first night we went out we encountered almost every species that lives in both rainforest and eucalypt forest in the tropics. We discovered Greater and Sugar Gliders and Brushtail Possums on the way to and from the rainforest and Lemuroid, Green and Herbert River Ringtail Possums in the rainforest.

It was immensely exciting being with someone who could teach me how and where to look. Those nights will always remain with me, nights filled with wonder and shining yellow eyes in a sea of inky black mystery.

Above, top left and clockwise: Cuscus; Greater Glider; Brushtail Possum; Sugar Glider; Feathertail Glider; Herbert River Ringtail Possum; Northern Pygmy Possum; Green Ringtail Possum. Centre: Greater Glider.

Sugar Glider.

THE REEF – A KALEIDOSCOPE OF LIVING THINGS

Dawn – strolling barefoot on wet squeaky sand with sea air caressing your body and the sounds of surf in your ears. The azure-blue sky melds with emerald green sea – and the birds!

Midday – snorkelling warm, shallow, crystal clear reef waters – diving over reef crests where waters turn to dark blue and schools of silver fish shimmer in the sunlight.

Sunset – watching orange skies blackened with shapes of flying birds returning from a day's fishing.

Sleepless nights dreaming as the subconscious mind craves another day. Days can become weeks and weeks months very quickly on the Great Barrier Reef; it is like one big happening, no space in between for boredom.

Unlike landscapes, which are predominantly filled with plants, underwater-scapes are comprised almost entirely of animals. There are corals, ascidians, sponges, anemones and hydroids – animals permanently fastened to the sea floor – a community of plankton snarers and trappers.

Then there are the fishes, masses of them with fraternities of plankton pickers, algae grazers, bottom grubbers, lurking and roving carnivores ... a kaleidoscope of living things, a fantasy in motion.

Above, top left and clockwise: Sponge; Striped Butterflyfish; Red-throated Emperor; Goatfish; Feather Seastar; Beaked Coralfish; Coral Cod and Seastar.

Blue Angelfish.

Above, top to bottom: Boxing Grey Kangaroos; Pied Oyster Catchers; Galahs; Pademelons and Crested Terns.

FACING THE CHALLENGE

There's
mystery
within those wild
yet not forgotten places

life,
ever-watchful, curious, yet aware,
tense to every sound and movement
behind, overhead, underfoot,
seeing yet unseen

busy,
lively, fussy, agile
all lightly making marks
and when gone
all that's left behind
is air

living things
rousing re-discovery.

Above, left to right: Darter; Crested Tern and Silver Gull.

Above, top to bottom, Hatching Green Turtle; Flycatcher; Grey Kangaroos, Crow and Silver Gulls.